Portraits of London

Geoffrey Fletcher

Kingsmead

Kingsmead Press
Rosewell House
Kingsmead Square
Bath

SBN 901571 95 4

Text set in 11/13 pt V.I.P. Palatino, printed by photolithography,
and bound in Great Britain at The Pitman Press, Bath

Contents

Introduction

Few people, I believe, nowadays read introductions. I used myself to do so – from over-conscientiousness, I suppose, – but gave it up on finding that I could never remember a word of them afterwards. The battery of dedications, forewords, prefaces and what not that cunning authors employed to swell the bulk, but not the sense, of an otherwise slight book was a favourite target for Swift's satire: such things are to modern readers merely the rind of the cheese. Still, I think it may be useful to make a very few remarks about the drawings in this book at the outset.

It is not, though it appears to be, a picture book – a relative of the Victorian gift book and its successor, the coffee table book of the 1960s. The subjects illustrated have been chosen with the greatest care so as to serve more than one kind of reader. To those who have not yet visited London, I hope it may suggest possibilities of study and exploration superior to the programme of the hard line tourists – those who only see what they have been told to see and even that in a mechanical, uncomprehending way totally destructive of all feeling or knowledge; to those who already know London, it may perhaps serve as a more useful kind of souvenir; and lastly, I hope it may awaken pleasurable recollections to those who once lived in London, but now live far away.

In common with many English cities and towns, London suffered much in the 1960s from land hungry developers and the ignorance and conceit of the so-called planner, whose only concern was for profit and prestige: it was the period of tower blocks of flats, supposedly efficient but actually life destroying, of giant offices of unholy aspect, of debauched High Streets and municipal fun factories, amusingly called leisure centres. But this toxic period produced its own antidote – an increasing awareness of the comelier, as well as the aesthetic, virtues of the older architecture and an increasing disbelief in the windy nonsense being served up as propaganda. The City of London, in particular, has had large areas totally ruined: Thames Street, for example, where the old warehouses and medieval river ways have been almost obliterated, and a petrol perfumed, concrete jungle substituted, a nightmare comparable only to the flat-lands of Nieuw Amsterdam or the outskirts of Milan or Rome. Fortunately, there is a good deal left in all parts of London, and of this I have chosen some lesser known aspects, including only a smaller proportion of those subjects that find their way on to postcards.

For my part, I seldom pay attention to the great views, the set pieces, either at home or abroad, but direct myself at once to the back alleys, where the barbers, haberdashers and shoemenders are, and the markets and churches visited but rarely, the quarters where washing hangs out over dead end kids. I admit I cannot imagine a new and more enterprising race of tourists who will come half way across the world to enthuse over the gritty streets of Lambeth or the peeling terraces of Islington and send home greetings from Seven Dials. Nevertheless, a wandering in less renowned quarters of London is undoubtedly rewarding, and therefore, as I have said above, it is to this end that I have tried, though gently, to incline the readers of this little book.

Many attempts have been made to analyse the fascination which the great city has over the minds of those who come to it, but London is by now far too complex to be either analysed or explained. It lacks the consistent grandeur of Rome, is less picturesque than Amsterdam, inferior in general beauty to Paris or Venice and considerably below Florence in elegance; yet, starting from a Roman port on the edge of the Western Sea, it has become the metropolis of the world. All one can do is to point out a few characteristics which, with many others, add up to its unique appeal; variety and vitality are certainly two of them.

"I often shed tears," said Charles Lamb, a thorough Londoner by birth and inclination, "in the motley Strand, for fulness of joy at so much life."

It seems to me that this is getting very close to the source of London's tremendous power: there is architecture of all periods; there are churches, stores, palaces, rivers, parks without number; but all this is only background stuff: why we really come to London is to get in touch with life, to share in a vivid sense of things happening, a feeling of being important, comprehensive, capable of prodigious activity, that for some reason is not obtainable elsewhere. Even London's history, which might be supposed to be fixed and incapable of change, has movement and elasticity about it. The recent discovery of a Roman signal station in Shadwell, close to the Highway (the old Ratcliff Highway, that might turn out to be a Roman riverside road), has revolutionised previous conceptions about the Roman river defences: the signal station was possibly one of a chain, stretching perhaps from Barking to the City, part of a highly organised defence system, hitherto unsuspected. So London's past, as well as its present, is alive. For the future, we may hope to apply to London the words in which Shakespeare described Cleopatra:

> "Age cannot wither her, nor custom stale
> Her infinite variety".

Whitehall

Whitehall has a dignified appearance very necessary to its function and an architectural unity which Palmerston refused to disturb. This was when he absolutely rejected Sir Gilbert Scott's design for the Foreign Office, and insisted on an Italianate design in harmony with the rest. The old belief that Scott adroitly revamped his scheme to do service as St. Pancras Station is quite false: the two elevations have little in common, and St. Pancras as we see it is much superior to the rejected Foreign Office designs. Under pressure, Scott produced a very creditable Foreign Office – the building in the middle distance of the drawing, on the right: the Treasury is at the far end, behind the trees, next comes Scott's Foreign Office and, on the right of the drawing, the Privy Council Offices.

The drawing was made from the Banqueting Hall – the only remaining fragment of Inigo Jones's great plan for a palace grandiose enough both to please Charles I and to exhaust his Exchequer. The Civil War put an end to it, as it did to Charles. Had the scheme prospered, London would possess perhaps the finest palace in Europe. The tragedy of Charles, of course, was that he was as much behind his age politically, as he was in advance of it as a patron of the arts.

Cardinal Cap Alley

Cardinal Cap Alley, Bankside

A charming alley, unexpectedly rural, where blackbirds sing in April, apparently untroubled by the surrounding industries of Bankside. But the pleasing old house, largely early nineteenth century, the back of which is seen in the drawing, has a fib on its forehead – an untruth foisted on it in the shape of a plaque on the front facing the river, placed there in the 1930s by a former occupier, who was possessed by the notion that Sir Christopher Wren once lived there. Wren, of course, never lived there, nor was he likely to, considering the rough, blackguardly character of Bankside in his time. Wren's friend, John Evelyn, castigates a so-called entertainment staged there, in which a poor horse was set on by vicious dogs. However, the idea has got into the heads of the guides of the riverboats, and hence it has become part of the apocryphal London-that-never-was.

Palace Gateway Richmond

Geoffrey Fletcher 1975

The Gateway, Richmond Palace

Richmond was originally called Sheen; Henry VII renamed it after his earldom of Richmond, Yorkshire, when rebuilding the palace, of which only a small portion now remains, and, of this, the Tudor gateway of mellow red brick is the most striking part. Queen Elizabeth slept here; in fact, she died at the palace in 1603. It was a favourite residence of hers during her long and spectacular reign. Georgian houses – the Trumpeter's House and Maids of Honour Row – form part of the precincts, and they harmonise well with the ancient fragment. Most of the palace was demolished and sold for building materials after the execution of Charles I.

TO LET
ROSE STREET
LAMB AND FLAG
SALOON BAR

The Lamb and Flag, Rose St., Covent Garden

The Lamb and Flag is one of the many pubs, full of character, that once served the great flower and vegetable market, now, with supreme contempt for continuity, life and atmosphere, removed to a dreary site at Nine Elms, where the atmosphere is at zero.

Until a few years ago, the facade of the Lamb and Flag was of early nineteenth century stucco, with a panel of the Agnus Dei in the centre, but though the front has been refaced, the picturesque interior of the pub remains unchanged in essentials. A history of the pub is displayed on the roof of the narrow alley alongside.

St Mary le Strand MARCH

St. Mary le Strand

St. Mary le Strand became islanded when the Strand was widened at the beginning of the twentieth century as part of the Aldwych Kingsway scheme, which demolished many ancient and interesting properties to make room for the infinitely boring and pompous classic of the Edwardian age. This, the last of the unhallowed depredations made on the churchyard, left St. Mary's with only its present day wedge shaped fore court, but many coffins remain undisturbed in the vaults below the church. There is not a more beautiful church in London than this masterpiece of James Gibbs. Its style, the fruit of Gibbs's education in Rome under Carlo Fontana, is best described as Baroque tinged with a hint of Rococo, but with a restraint derived from Wren and the English tradition and the essential reasonableness of the doctrine of the Church of England.

W J WOODWARD FISHER
Duke Shore
Limehouse

Duke Shore, Limehouse

Though so much life has departed from the industrial Thames, some barge building and repairing still goes on in Limehouse. At one time, and indeed within living memory, the entire waterfront was peopled by those who gained their living off – and on – the river. Whistler's etchings and old paintings and photographs show how fascinating this part of the river was in the nineteenth century, when shipwrights, ships' chandlers and the like lived above their premises in a riparian community, now only a ghost of its former self.

All this riverside life has its memorial in Dickens's late novel, "Our Mutual Friend": The Grapes pub (the building with the bow window towards the left of the drawing) appears in his pages as the "Six Jolly Fellowship Porters"; fortunately, it remains very much as the novelist knew it – unsophisticated, therefore unspoilt.

BRADLEYS BAR
HANWAY STREET

Hanway Street

Hanway Street, one of London's many back alleys, does not, as I once imagined, commemorate Jonas Hanway, the umbrella man. Hanway is a corruption of "The Hand-Way", a country lane in the Elizabethan period, now connecting Tottenham Court Road with Oxford Street, the latter itself a country road up to the middle of the eighteenth century.

Cast iron bollards are a feature of Hanway Street, which also includes among its items of interest the back (the only remaining part) of the once famous Frascati's Restaurant, which, like Romano's in the Strand, survived, though diminished in glory, until the early 1950s.

OFFICES
TO LET
CONRAD RITB
Embassy
SHOE REPAIRS
SUSSEX
ALL ONE PRICE
TO LET
CONRAD RITB
SHOE REPAIRS
Crown 1976
Passage

Crown Passage, St. James's

Opposite Marlborough House is the Pall Mall entrance to Crown Passage, originally Crown Court, a choice specimen of the London by-way, running from Pall Mall to King Street and dating from 1673. In the 1930s, it possessed a chimney sweep's establishment, as well as a rag and bottle emporium; these have now gone, but a varied selection of shops remains, forming, as it were, a narrow market with a distinctly village-like atmosphere. There is the Red Lion, a charming Regency pub, at the Pall Mall end, and there are gas lamps, picturesque survivors from the chimney sweeping era, giving the precise artistic completion to this most delightful of narrow ways.

The Palace of Westminster

A Royal Palace, for that is what it is officially, has stood here for a thousand years. The present Palace of Westminster – the Houses of Parliament, as we prefer to call it – is the masterpiece of A. W. N. Pugin and Sir Charles Barry. Pugin was responsible for the decorative part, inside and outside of the great building, from pinnacles down to inkstands, clothing, as it were, with Perpendicular detail the mass planned by Barry. It replaced the old palace which was destroyed by fire, all but Westminster Hall and St. Stephen's Chapel. The new building came in for much contemporary criticism, but its quality is now accepted beyond doubt, and the truth is that it has become stamped into the minds not merely of Londoners, but also of the entire English race.

St Paul, Covent Garden

St. Paul's, Covent Garden

"The handsomest barn in Europe", as its architect, Inigo Jones, described it to his client, the Duke of Bedford, St. Paul's has been the spiritual heart of Covent Garden for three centuries. It has been associated with the stage since Garrick worshipped there, and an ever growing number of theatrical personalities are commemorated inside – Marie Lloyd, Charles Cochran, Ada Reeve and José Collins among them. But a greater than these lived in the parish: on the north wall is the memorial to William and Mary Ann Turner, erected by J. M. W. Turner in 1832 and remarkable for the pleonasm in the first line of the inscription, "beneath and near this place"; Turner, mighty as he was in art, was no literary gent.

In the portico on the market side of the church, Professor Higgins first met Eliza Dolittle and Mr. Pepys watched the Punch and Judy show on its arrival in England.

TO LET

The Monument

The Monument commemorates the Great Fire of London, which began close by in Pudding Lane on Sunday, 2nd September, 1666, damaging or destroying 87 churches and over 13,000 houses. The wonder is that London could so quickly recover itself after this and the disastrous plague of the previous year. The Roman Doric coursed column, 202 feet high, was designed by Wren to serve also as a telescope; this purpose was abandoned because of the London smoke.

The Monument was built 1671–77. Its podium is thoroughly Roman with a Latin inscription and a Roman type bas relief of allegorical figures attending Charles II, the monarch being heroically clad in Roman armour, though wearing a full bottomed wig.

Clink Street Bankside

Clink Street

This portion of Bankside, along the riverside from the old inn, the Anchor, through winding ways to Southwark Cathedral, retains its character intact, at least at the time of writing: one never knows when vandalistic modern requirements will destroy its harmony. Piranesi-like is Clink Street, under the damp, grey arches; here once stood the Clink Prison – used for the confinement of Dissenters before the passing of the Toleration Act – from which is derived the English slang term, now an archaism, for a gaol.

Beyond Clink Wharf is all that survives of the Palace of the Bishops of Winchester, built in the first half of the fourteenth century – chiefly the remains of the Great Hall with a fine rose window of the Decorated period, damaged like the rest of the Palace in the great Southwark fire.

Cheshire Cheese
TRATTORIA
VAL CENO
FULLY LICENSED
Fleet St. June 1977

Fleet Street: Put Out More Flags

Fleet Street is a village with two parish churches; a population consisting mostly of writers and journalists has been settled there for the last three centuries, and its cottage industry is the production of newspapers. A list of writers who at one time or other have worked in Fleet Street would include almost all the considerable figures in English literature, from Ben Jonson up to the present time. With so many writers about, taverns naturally abound, but the only old one remaining is the Cheshire Cheese, rebuilt after the Fire. Its lamp hangs out over Fleet Street, though the entrance is down Wine Office Court, where Goldsmith once lived. Kate Greenaway's father, a wood engraver, had his office also in the Court in a house which, until the bombing, was a part of the terrace on the side opposite the Cheshire Cheese. Ben Jonson and his friends gathered at the Devil Tavern, where Child's Bank now stands.

The Post Office occupies the site of the Mitre, a tavern made famous by Dr. Johnson's patronage.

There are, however, other items of interest in Fleet Street besides the writers – the clock with the giants at St. Dunstan's, for example – referred to by Byron, Cowper, Dickens and Lamb among others – the contemporary statue of Queen Elizabeth above the old school door in St. Dunstan's churchyard – El Vino's wine establishment with its rich late Victorian interior, where you must wear a collar and tie – the old Jacobean house called Prince Henry's Room – and many more. Over all is the great dome of St. Paul's.

The drawing shows Fleet Street in an unusual dress, the trappings of the 1977 Silver Jubilee.

July 1977
Gateway - Lincoln's Inn

Gateway, Lincoln's Inn

On each side of Fleet Street are three of the Inns of Court – the Inner and Middle Temple on the south and Lincoln's Inn on the north – all with ancient buildings, lawns, great old trees and gardens, forming places of retreat and renewal not only for their proprietors, but also for the general public, who are not excluded from these collegiate pleasures. ". . . . . . . inns of court with their learned air, and hall, and butteries, just like Cambridge colleges," as Charles Lamb noted.

The old hall of Lincoln's Inn, dating from the Tudor period, is where the Chancery action of Jarndyce v. Jarndyce was held in "Bleak House". The New Hall, an admirable example of Gothic Revival Perpendicular/Tudor is, like the gateway illustrated here, part of the work of the 1840s by Philip Hardwicke.

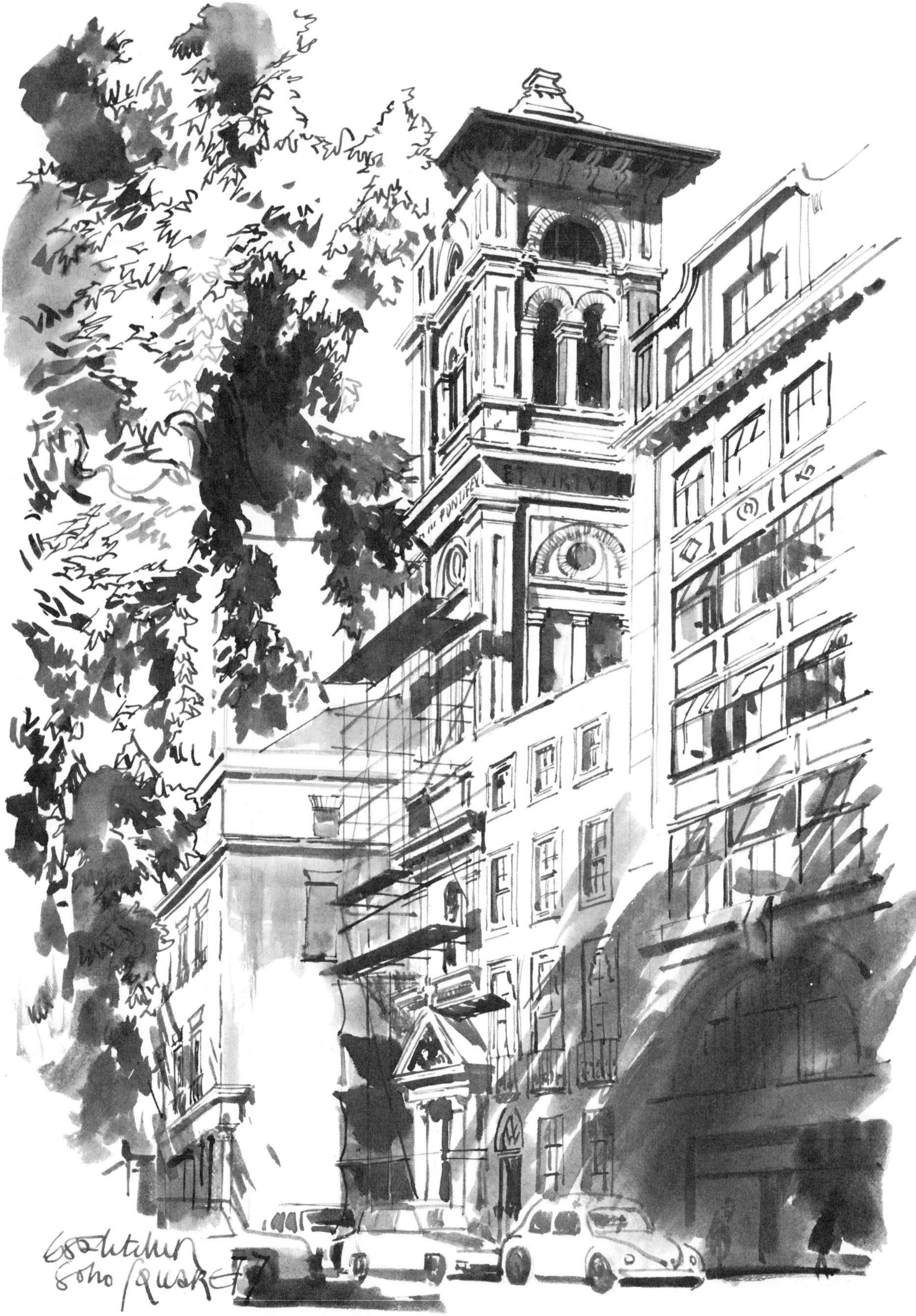
PONTIFEX
ET VIRTVT

St. Patrick's, Soho Square

London has for centuries past found a home for foreigners and foreign words that are prepared to behave themselves, both the capital and its speech showing remarkable powers of assimilation and naturalisation. Soho is London's oldest foreign quarter. Its chief open space, Soho Square (originally Monmouth Square), was laid out in the reign of Charles II; a much eroded statue of the monarch by Cibber, sculptor of the bas relief on the Monument, stands in the centre. Though much rebuilt in the 1920s and 1930s, a few of the old houses remain in the square, one being the presbytery attached to St. Patrick's Church. St. Patrick's itself, originally projected for the local Irish Roman Catholic population, belongs to the 1890s. The church is not architecturally remarkable, but its red brick campanile gives a suitable Italian touch to this largely Italian quarter.

PASSMORE STREET SW1
GRAHAM TERRACE SW1
FOX & HOUNDS
Pimlico

The Fox and Hounds, Passmore Street, Pimlico

This small pub, recently under threat of demolition – a threat happily now lifted, is a true London local. It serves a number of streets of small terraced houses, in many of which the same families have lived for generations, all on the Grosvenor Estate. Such streets of artisans' dwellings form the greatest contrast to the magnificent Eaton and Grosvenor Squares, yet the principle underlying them all is the same – a respect for harmony of proportion and seemliness of effect that makes these Pimlico streets so satisfying a place in which to wander on a summer day in London.

The Grenadier
Wilton Row

The Grenadier

The most interesting approach to the Grenadier is down the cobbled, winding Grosvenor Crescent Mews. A mews was originally a place where falcons were kept; in later centuries, horses took over, to be followed by cars and taxis in the twentieth century. But the ponies and horses that appear in Rotten Row are still stabled in Grosvenor Crescent Mews. The Grenadier, a relic of the Waterloo period, is one of London's most interesting pubs. A flight of worn stone steps leads to the door, and the facade is shadowed by a great tree and the canopy of a grape vine in the summer time. These steps and the high windows set between wooden pilasters infilled by panelling give a character much resembling the old houses of Amsterdam to the place, which was originally an officers' mess.

Opposite, in Old Barrack Yard, is the Duke of Wellington's mounting block; the Regency buildings with the archway leading to Grosvenor Crescent Mews were part of his stables. The Grenadier (formerly called The Guardsman) is said to be haunted during September by the ghost of an officer who was accidentally flogged to death after being caught cheating at cards.

York Water Gate

The York Water Gate

The York Water Gate originally stood on the river's brink – the Thames before the construction of the Victoria Embankment covered the site now occupied by the promenade and gardens – so that the Water Gate is now high and dry and landlocked. It is the only surviving part of York House, once the residence of the Archbishops of York and later of the Dukes of Buckingham: Francis Bacon was born there in 1561. The water gate was built in 1626, at which time it must have given a richly Venetian touch to the duke's riverside mansion. Both Inigo Jones and Nicholas Stone have been credited with its design. As it is very characteristic of Jones's treatment of Renaissance mouldings and orders, it is almost certainly designed by him, but probably carried out by Stone under his directions.

Cleopatra's Needle

Cleopatra's Needle

Cleopatra's Needle, a monolith of red granite weighing 180 tons, is probably London's most famous antiquity, apart from our home produced Tower of London. It was erected at Heliopolis by Thothmes III about 1500 B.C. and later removed to Alexandria. On each of the Needle's four sides are lateral inscriptions added by Rameses II (generally believed to be the Pharaoh of the Exodus) to celebrate his victories: only the central hieroglyphs are by Thothmes. It was given to the English nation early in the nineteenth century, and eventually brought here in a specially constructed ship, "The Cleopatra", – not without incident, for she went adrift for a time in the Bay of Biscay – and set up on its present site in 1878. In the porch of Holy Trinity Church, Tulse Hill, are two massive chairs made from the wood of the raft on which the obelisk was floated down the Thames.

Hoop and Grapes
Bass Charrington

The Hoop and Grapes, Aldgate

The Hoop and Grapes, Aldgate, one of London's oldest taverns, is one of a group of three ancient houses that is the only remaining fragment of the medieval Butchers Row, a picturesque shambles or butchering place that survived more of less intact until the end of the last century. Defoe refers to Butchers Row in his powerful narrative, "A Journal of the Plague Year", for the deaths in Aldgate and Whitechapel reached awe inspiring proportions during the height of the plague, the area having been let off comparatively lightly prior to those months of July and August, 1665.

By the Same Author

The London Nobody Knows
Geoffrey Fletcher's London
City Sights
London Overlooked
Pearly Kingdom
London after Dark
London's River
London's Pavement Pounders
Down Among the Meths Men
The London Dickens Knew
Italian Impressions
London Souvenirs
Elements of Sketching
Sketching in Colour
Changing London
Offbeat in London
Offbeat in the City
Guide to Dickens's London
Sketching in Black and White
Painting in Oil
Painting in Water Colour

Sets of Prints

The London You Love
City Churches
My London
The Tidal Thames
The Upper Thames
London in Colour